D1742503

Adventure Story Bible
Book 11

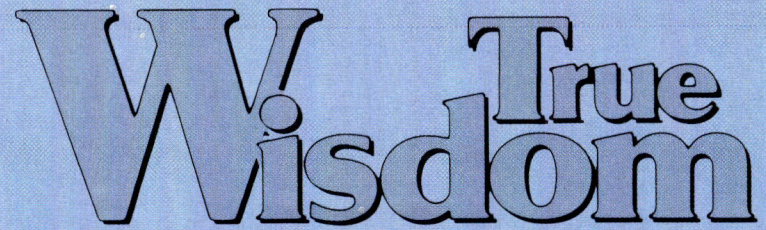

True
Wisdom

Written by Anne de Graaf

Illustrated by José Pérez Montero

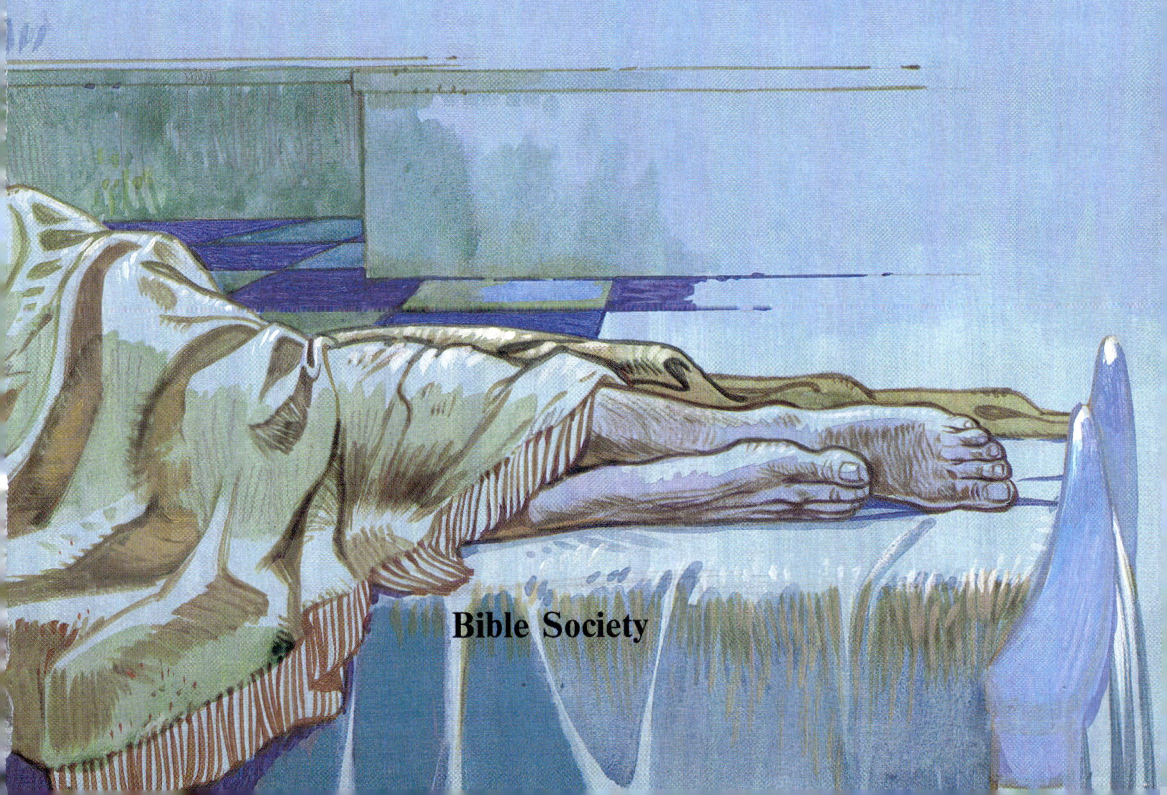

Bible Society

True Wisdom

Contents − 1 Kings 1−4, 6−12; 1 Chronicles 22, 28−29;
2 Chronicles 1−11; Psalm 72; Proverbs; Song of Songs;
Ecclesiastes

Book 11 — Bible background

What is wisdom? Is it knowing answers to questions and being clever, or is it more than that? Where do you find wisdom? These questions are explored in the Books of Proverbs and Ecclesiastes. They give us sayings which are helpful for us all whenever and wherever we live.

King Solomon was King David's son, and one of the wisest kings that ever lived. His wisdom was a gift from God. He had a keen knowledge of how people thought and what they felt. He also understood a great deal about the world around him, animals, plants, and the sea. Kings from all over the world sent people to Solomon's court to learn from him. Jerusalem became famous because of his great learning.

Like his father King David, Solomon wrote poetry and songs, and also wise sayings. His words were repeated from parents to children for many hundreds of years as examples of how life should be lived. This wisdom still applies today — wisdom which is knowledge and good judgement.

The Hebrew Bible says that the Song of Songs was written by Solomon. It may have been written about him or dedicated to him. The Song of Songs is a collection of songs about love and longing. Jewish people often think of it as a picture of the relationship between God and his people, and Christians as a picture of the relationship between Christ and the Church.

It is not clear who wrote Ecclesiastes, although it has often been linked with Solomon. In it the writer explores what life is about. In doing this he raises questions which people are still asking today, such as "Why am I here? What is life about? What really matters in life?" Ecclesiastes shows us that life without God is really no life at all.

Solomon lived a full life. He was king of a great kingdom and had wealth, love, power, and glory. He also had wisdom and knowledge, and God gave him a long life. With God's help Solomon promised to follow the teachings of God, and to love the Lord with all his heart, just as his father David had. But when Solomon became older he broke that promise. He chose not to do what God wanted, but trusted instead in his own power and wisdom. Yet God remembered his promise to David that he would always love his descendants, so God didn't reject Solomon as king.

It is not clear whether Solomon is behind the wisdom in Proverbs and Ecclesiastes or the poetry of the Song of Songs, but this *Adventure Story Bible* book retells the wisdom found in these books in such a way as to link it with Solomon. It also retells some of the wisdom as stories, to make it easier to understand. Through seeking and following this wisdom we are brought closer to God, the source of all wisdom.

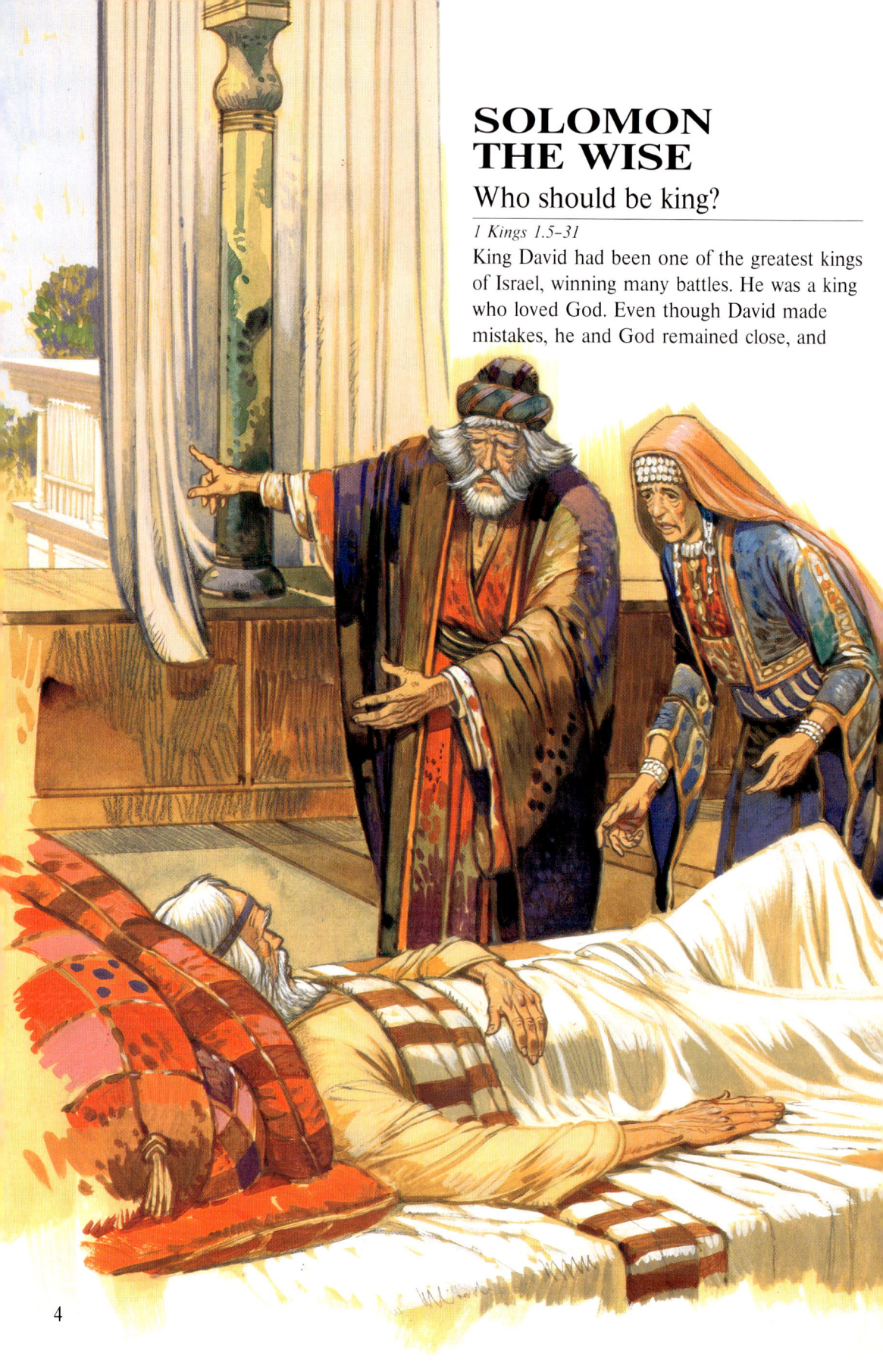

SOLOMON THE WISE

Who should be king?

1 Kings 1.5–31

King David had been one of the greatest kings of Israel, winning many battles. He was a king who loved God. Even though David made mistakes, he and God remained close, and

God promised to look after David's descendants for ever.

When King David was a very old man all the people in the kingdom wondered who would take his place. They knew he was very ill and would probably die soon. David had many sons, but the eldest was Adonijah. He was a fine-looking and popular young man.

Adonijah said, "I am next in line for the throne. I will make myself king. David is so old, there is nothing he can do about it."

Adonijah gathered together many fighting men, and provided chariots for them to ride in. He invited princes, priests, and generals to come to a feast at which he intended to be proclaimed king. But Adonijah didn't invite anyone who didn't want him to be king.

David had already made it clear that his son Solomon should be king after him. God had also said through the prophet Nathan that Solomon was his choice. So Nathan thought to himself, "I had better do something quickly, or Adonijah really will become king, and then he will have us all killed."

Nathan called Bathsheba, Solomon's mother, and together they thought of a plan. Bathsheba went to visit King David in his bedroom where he was resting.

"Please your Majesty," she said to David, "didn't you promise in the Lord's name that Solomon would be king after you? Your son

Adonijah has made himself king and is already holding a feast to celebrate."

Then Nathan came into the room. "Tell me, my lord, is this something you have done without letting us know?" he asked.

David answered, "I tell you in the name of the Lord that I knew nothing about this. Solomon is to become king in my place." David had been caught off guard. He knew he would have to do something quickly.

Solomon becomes king

1 Kings 1.32–53; 2.25–26, 34

David called together Zadok the priest, Nathan the prophet, and one of his generals. "Anoint Solomon as king," he ordered. "He will reign instead of me. Then let all the people rejoice and hold a feast to celebrate the new king."

"It shall be done," said his general. So they anointed Solomon as king, then went into Jerusalem and sounded the trumpets, spreading the word that David had chosen a new king.

When Adonijah and his guests heard the trumpet blasts in the city, they wondered what had happened. A messenger came and told Adonijah that the people were celebrating because Solomon had been made the new king! Adonijah's guests slipped away as quickly as they could. They didn't want to be accused of being traitors to the new king.

King Solomon heard that Adonijah was afraid of him, and sent for him. Adonijah begged for mercy. "Please, great King Solomon, don't kill me. You're the king now, everyone can see that," Adonijah said.

Solomon said, "If you are loyal to me then I will have no reason to kill you, but if you are not, you will die."

But Adonijah once more tried to take some power from Solomon, so Solomon had him killed. Solomon made sure that no one questioned his kingship. He was David's choice and the Lord's choice.

The young king

1 Kings 3.2–5; 2 Chronicles 1.7

When David died, all Israel mourned for him. He had been a great king, and the people had loved him. Now David was gone, young Solomon suddenly felt very much alone. He would have to decide many important things for his people, and that would not be easy.

To be a king with gold and jewels, eat the best food and wear the best clothes sounds like a good life. But to be a king who knows what is best for the people is very hard. When David died and Solomon was king, he didn't feel very sure of himself.

Every day Solomon wished he could say, "I don't know" to the ministers, generals, priests, and people who asked his advice. "But a king cannot say that," he thought to himself.

David had told Solomon to follow the Lord, and to be fair and just with the people. Solomon wondered how he was going to become the good king that David had asked him to be.

Then one night, Solomon had a dream. God appeared to him and said, "Ask whatever you wish from me, and I will give it to you."

Some people might have asked for more possessions, good health, more money, or power. Solomon did not ask for any of these things. Instead he wanted something far better.

Solomon's dream

1 Kings 3.6–15; 2 Chronicles 1.8–13

When God asked Solomon to make a wish he answered, "Lord, you helped my father David while he was king because he trusted in you. Now you have made me king in his place, even though I'm very young. I don't know how to be a good king like my father David. I only ask for this one thing. Give me a heart full of wisdom, so that I can see what is right and wrong and rule over your people as you want. Help me to judge your people with wisdom. Help me to know the difference between good and bad."

This answer pleased God very much. He said to Solomon, "I will give you a wise heart.

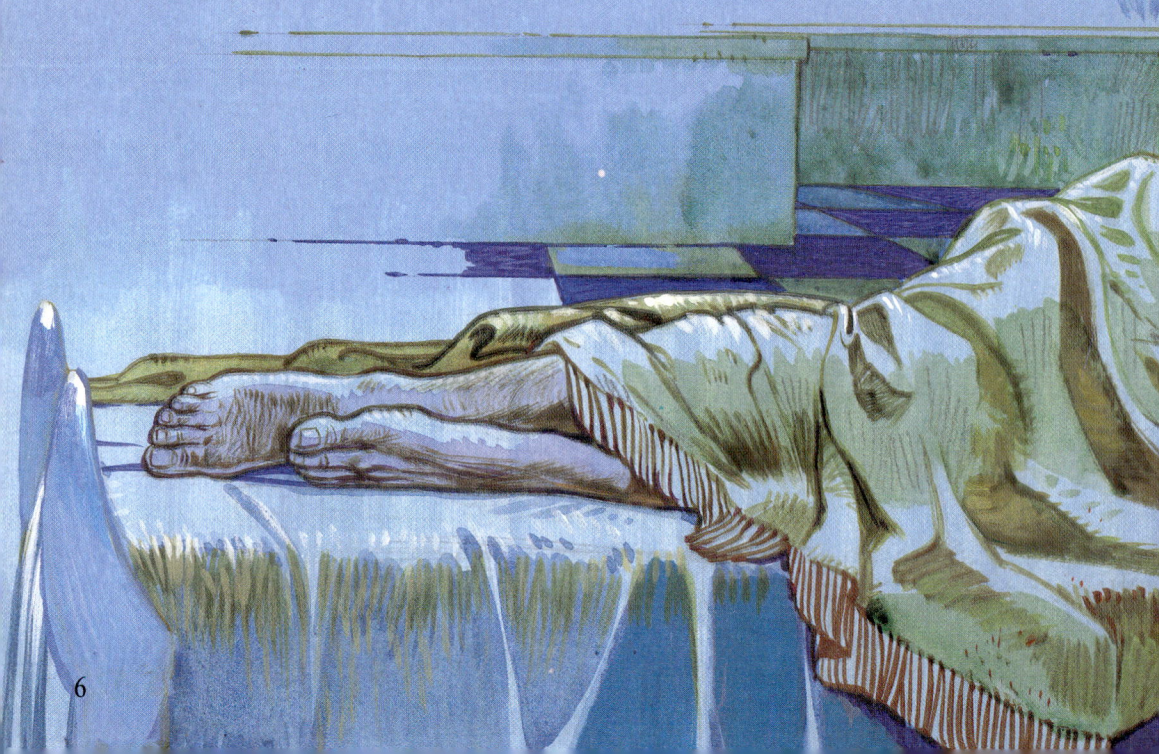

There will never be a king as wise or as great as you. Because you have asked for this, and have not asked to live a long life or become rich, I will give these other things to you as well. You will have riches and honour, and if you do what I tell you I will see that you live a long life."

Then Solomon woke up and realized that God had spoken to him in the dream. He went to Jerusalem and stood before the Lord's Covenant Box, which contained the Ten Commandments. There he thanked the Lord for what he had promised. Then he held a great feast for all his officials. The reign of Solomon the wise had begun!

The baby with two mothers

1 Kings 3.16–28

God gave Solomon a wise heart which helped him as he judged the people. This is a story which shows how wise he was.

It is about two mothers. One day they came to King Solomon, each carrying a baby. The first woman's baby was dead, and the second woman's baby was alive. They put the babies on the floor at the foot of Solomon's throne.

"Your Majesty," the first woman said, "I live in the same house as this woman. She and I both had babies within a few days of each other. One night this woman's baby died. She got up in the middle of the night, crept into my room, and took my son while I was asleep! Then she put her dead son by my side.

"When I woke up the next morning, I saw this dead baby in bed with me." She pointed to the lifeless child at Solomon's feet. "But when I looked closely, I saw he was not mine, but hers!"

Then the second woman said, "No! She's lying. The living baby is my son, and the dead one is hers!"

Solomon watched as the women shouted at each other. "The living baby is mine!"

"No! He's mine!"

"You're wrong! He's mine!"

Solomon raised his hand for silence. "Both of these women claim the living baby as her own. Guard, take the baby and raise your sword!"

Everyone in the hall wondered, "What will the king do?"

The king said, "Cut the living child in two. Then give half to one woman and half to the other." The people gasped. But Solomon didn't really mean to have the baby cut in half. This was his way of finding out the truth.

The first woman covered her mouth with her hands to stop herself from screaming. "No! Please don't kill him. Oh, my lord, give her the baby. Then at least he'll stay alive."

But the second woman said, "You're right, your Majesty. Go on, cut him in half! Then neither of us will have him! Go on, cut him in two!"

The king sighed and told his guard to lower his sword. "Give the living baby to the first woman. She spoke the truth and is the child's real mother. Only the true mother could have spoken as you did."

Solomon knew that the woman who had shown a mother's love for the baby must be his mother. When all Israel heard this story they were filled with respect and awe for their wise king. It was clear to everyone that he had wisdom from God.

TRUE WISDOM
Loving and obeying the Lord

Proverbs 10.27; 14.26–27; 15.16–33; 16.6; 19.23; 22.4

Solomon wrote that there is only one way to make sure you do what is right. That is to love the Lord and obey him. Solomon wanted people to take God seriously, and to try and live as he wanted.

Solomon often taught by giving examples of what would happen to people who lived as God would like them to, and what would happen to those who didn't. "If you love and obey the Lord," he wrote, "then you can be sure that God will be with you and help you. But he will not help people who do evil and hurt others. God will cut their lives short."

Respecting and believing in God helps us to live good and enjoyable lives. Following God's rules for living will keep us from a great deal of trouble in this world. That's because God knows who we are and what is best for us.

Solomon, who was one of the richest men who ever lived, said it was better to love and obey the Lord than to have gold and jewels. He said that the Lord hears the prayers of those who try to find out what he wants.

Solomon gave the people some good advice. "Good people," he said, "think before they open their mouths, but bad people say whatever comes into their heads."

"A happy smile will make others happy, too, and telling people good news will make them feel good."

"If you have done something wrong and others tell you about it, don't be upset or ignore them. Listen, and you will grow and learn."

When you love and obey God, you will enjoy a good life. You will know that God loves you and forgives you when you do wrong things. He will help you to be safe and secure. These are wise words! Loving the Lord and wanting to learn are the first steps towards true wisdom.

The wise man and the fool

Proverbs 10.8, 13–14, 23; 12.1, 15–16, 23; 13.14–16, 20; 14.1, 3, 7–8, 15–18, 24, 33; 15.5, 7, 14, 20–21; 16.16, 21–23; 17.10, 12, 16, 24, 28; 18.2, 6–7, 15; 19.25, 29; 21.22; 22.3

To teach people how much the success or failure of their lives depends on themselves, Solomon talked about two different types of people.

Once there were two men. One was wise and the other was a fool. The wise man respected God and tried to shape his life around what God wanted for him. But the foolish man went his own way. He didn't care whom he hurt, or how. He did his own thing. The foolish man chose not to listen to God. Nor did he listen to the advice of older people who knew more than he did.

This man became wise because, when he was young, he listened to what he was told. He respected his parents. He thought before he said or did anything. Whenever he learnt something new, he wanted to know more. He never gave up because something was hard. He enjoyed his work and felt happy with what he had done.

The wise man spent his time with other people who loved God and tried their best to do what he wanted. They had a lot in common and could share with each other many good things. He knew enough to stay away from bad people who would try to get him to do bad things. The wise man chose his friends carefully, and stayed out of trouble.

The foolish man, however, never listened when people warned him that what he was doing would bring him trouble. He said, "I don't want other people to tell me what to do! I'll do whatever I want! I don't care if I learn or not."

The foolish man never thought about what he was doing, he just didn't care. He didn't think before acting. Too often he did something even before he knew whether or not it was a good idea.

The foolish man had troublemakers and hooligans for friends. He didn't try to stop them doing wrong, but joined in. He would go out with them, get drunk, and often end up in fights. He may have had more friends than the wise man, but none of the foolish man's friends helped him when he was in trouble. The foolish man liked nothing better than to talk about himself, and he was lazy.

It is up to us to choose which sort of life we would like to live.

The good and the bad

Proverbs 10.3, 6-7, 11, 20-21, 24-25; 11.23; 12.5-7, 10; 13.25; 14.11; 15.8-9; 17.15; 21.3, 26

When people are accused of doing something wrong they are either guilty or innocent. That means they either did the bad thing, or they did not. The man who steals money has done a wrong thing, and hurt someone else. The man who spends his money thoughtfully, and is generous, is a good man.

Solomon taught about two types of people – those who do bad, and those who do good. People need to choose which sort of person they would like to be.

There once was a good man. He was wise enough to know he should stay away from bad people. He stayed out of trouble and brought happiness to the people around him. God loved him and took care of him.

People learnt from what the good man said. He wanted only what was best. He took care of his animals and was kind to people, even if they had not been kind to him. The good man was content and happy, not always wishing for things he did not have.

The good man was able to keep going, even when times were hard. Whether he lived in a tent or a palace, his home was a happy one. The Lord loved to hear the prayers of the good man. When he died, the people who had known him had good memories of him.

The bad man, however, did not think about what he did, so he often made mistakes and did wrong things. He didn't know how to choose good friends. He lied and became wicked. God grew angry with this man.

When the bad man's behaviour brought him trouble, he was scared and went into hiding. One day the trouble he caused would catch up with him, and he would realize that this was not a good way to live.

Laziness and hard work

Proverbs 10.4-5, 26; 12.11, 24; 13.4; 14.23; 18.9; 19.15; 21.25; 22.13

Some people work hard, and some people are lazy. This story is based on what the book of Proverbs says can happen to each type of person.

There once was a boy who was given everything he wanted. Whatever he asked for he was given right away, even if it wasn't good for him. Whatever he wanted to do he was allowed to do.

In the same town there lived a girl. She was the same age as the boy, but otherwise they were quite different. When she asked for new toys or clothes, her parents sometimes got them for her, but often they didn't. When they didn't, her parents explained that it would not be good for her to get everything she wanted.

When this girl was naughty, her parents punished her because they loved her and wanted her to grow up knowing the difference between right and wrong. Afterwards, when she was sorry, they held her tight and hugged her. Then she felt new inside, and knew she was loved.

When the girl grew older her parents said, "Do you want to learn to be our helper? You can do little jobs around the house. We're all members of the same family, so let's help each other." Sometimes the girl helped her father and sometimes she helped her mother. Either way, she learnt how to help others and to do a good job.

As the boy grew older he became angrier and grumpier. Even though he had all he could ever want, he was never satisfied. Nor was he willing to learn anything from his parents or teachers.

Eventually the boy grew into a man. When it was time for him to work for a living, he wouldn't. He was too lazy. He did nothing all day but complain and sleep.

"I don't want to work!" he would say. "Leave me alone, today's my day off!"

"Every day can't be your day off," his family would tell him. "Come on now, it's time you tried to get a job."

After a long time his father found someone who would employ him, but the young man was careless at work and broke many valuable things. The man he worked for said, "I would be better off without him."

The man eventually became a beggar because no one would employ him, and he didn't want to work anyway. "Why should I work?" he said. "I might get hurt on the job!"

What little money the lazy man did get from begging, he spent on worthless things instead of on food, so he was always hungry.

The young woman, however, knew the value of hard work. She had learnt how to do several things very well. Not everything had come easily to her, but when she had failed, she kept trying until she had learnt whatever she needed to know.

This woman listened to the advice of other wise people. She saved her money and gave much of it away to the poor and hungry.

She lived a long and fulfilling life. People respected her and she grew wise. When she died, everyone who had known her talked about her goodness for many years afterwards. The man, however, died young. No one knew where he died, and no one cared.

The power of words

Proverbs 10.18–19, 31–32; 11.9, 11–14; 12.6, 17–19, 22;13.2–3; 14.5, 25; 15.1–2, 4; 16.1, 24; 17.27

What are the differences between hurtful and thoughtless words, which are spoken in anger, and considered, caring words, which are spoken in kindness? One sort hurts, while the other makes you feel good.

Suppose someone said to you, "Thank you. You're fun to be with, and I like you." How would you feel? You would probably smile, and it would do you the world of good! It would help you to love others, too.

But what if someone said, "Get lost! You're ugly and stupid – I don't like you." That would hurt. It would make you want to hurt the person who said it, and maybe other people, too.

Some of the wisest advice King Solomon ever gave was about the power of words. He said that words can make all the difference to a person, and we need to be careful to use the right ones.

Solomon said that if you talk too much, sooner or later you will say something which hurts someone else. Anyone who talks about other people behind their backs is a fool. The man who speaks the truth is wise.

Solomon spoke about a man who did not worship God, and destroyed his best friend with the words he spoke against him. He made up stories and told lies.

Solomon said that the words of good people build others up, encourage them, and make them feel strong. The words of wise people can bring healing. The good person is a peace-maker. The Lord loves people who are fair and do not lie.

"Beware of the dangerous man who speaks violent words, and who is always arguing and shouting," Solomon said. He taught that the best way to answer someone who is angry is to calm them with a gentle word. "Don't shout," he said, "it only makes the other person much more angry."

The family

Proverbs 10.1; 12.4; 13.1, 24; 17.21, 25; 18.22; 19.13–14,18, 27; 20.11; 22.6, 15

When Solomon was king he had many wives and many children. Because he had such a large family, he learnt first-hand how important it is to have wisdom when taking care of a family. Solomon's wisdom can be just as helpful now as it was then.

Families always have good times and bad times. Solomon said that a wife is a blessing from God. She shouldn't make her husband ashamed of her, and she shouldn't nag. A wife who nags all the time sounds like water going drip-drip-drip.

If children want to make their parents proud they should listen to advice. A foolish child will do nothing but make his mother cry. Children who stop listening to their parents are foolish.

Parents show their love for their children by correcting them when they do bad things. If they really love their children, they should show them what is bad and what is good. If they don't, their children will have great difficulties later on in life.

But parents should only punish their children because they want to teach them, not because they have run out of patience and are in a bad mood.

Solomon told parents that if they bring up their children to learn about God and point them in the right direction early on, they will continue on the right path all their lives.

SOLOMON THE BUILDER
David's last wish

1 Chronicles 22.6–19; 28.11–20; 29.1–20, 28

Solomon was famous for his wisdom. But there were also other things which made him famous. One was the temple Solomon built for people to worship God in.

Before David died he gave Solomon the job he had dreamt of doing himself. That was to build a temple for the Lord. David had paid for the land where the temple would be built, and had drawn up plans for how he wanted the temple to look. He had saved a massive fortune in gold, silver, and bronze, all of which he wanted to use on building the great temple for God.

But God had told David that he would not be the one to build the temple — that would be Solomon's job. Before David had died he had given his son exact instructions on how it should be done.

The temple of the Lord would be magnificent, filled with gold and precious stones. It was to be built with all the best materials, including precious cedar wood from Lebanon. Solomon hired the best craftsmen from foreign countries. Nothing was too good for the house of God.

The people helped in every way they could. Just before David died he gave yet one more huge gift towards the building of the temple. The people did the same. Giving towards the building of the temple made David and the people feel very happy. They knew they were giving to God from what he had given them. David died in peace, knowing that his wish for a temple for the Lord would come true in the coming years.

A temple for the Lord

1 Kings 6.1–38; 8.1–9.9; 2 Chronicles 2.1–7.22

The temple of God took seven years to build.
It would last four hundred years. It was

divided into three parts, with the innermost room being the most special. That was the place for the Lord's Covenant Box, which contained the commandments given by God to Moses.

Cedar wood and gold covered the temple, inside and out. The best metal workers, artists, and sculptors from all the surrounding lands made beautiful figures and designs to cover the ceiling and walls.

When the temple was finished, Solomon called together all the people of Israel. The priests brought the Covenant Box into the temple and put it in the special room. Suddenly the temple was filled with a cloud shining with the dazzling light of the Lord's presence. God's glory and power were so great, the priests couldn't even do their duties inside the temple. All the people knew that the Lord was very close to them.

Then Solomon prayed, "God, thank you that I was able to build this temple for you, and that my father David planned it. But even this temple is not worthy of you. No place is big or high enough to contain you who made the earth and the sky. Lord, when your people are stubborn or bad, if they come here and pray, saying they are sorry, please forgive them. Let this temple be a place where men and women can always find you."

Then Solomon and the priests made sacrifices to the Lord. They offered their crops and animals from their flocks as a way of giving back to God what he had given to them. For two whole weeks the entire land had a feast. The people ate and drank and praised God, because now they had a proper place which could be called God's house.

Afterwards God appeared to Solomon. He said, "If you obey my laws and serve honestly in all you do, I will do what I promised your father, David. I will live among the people of Israel, and make this temple my home. I will listen to the prayers of the people who come here. But if you abandon me I will leave this place, and bring disaster upon it."

The kingdom of Solomon

1 Kings 4.20–28; 7.1–12; 9.10–28; 10.14–29; 2 Chronicles 1.14–17; 8.1–18; 9.13–28; Psalm 72

When God gave Solomon wisdom, he also blessed him with a great kingdom. Because his father David had fought and won so many wars, Solomon ruled during a time of peace. He was able to build up his kingdom and did not have to worry so much about fighting wars.

As well as the temple for the Lord, Solomon also built a magnificent palace for himself, made of cedar, stone, and bronze. This palace took thirteen years to complete. His throne was made of ivory and gold, and decorated with statues of lions. There was no other throne like it in all the world.

Then he built a beautiful palace for his wife, the daughter of the king of Egypt. Solomon needed many workers for these building projects. All the men who belonged to former enemy tribes became Solomon's workers, and his own people helped according to their skill.

Solomon also ordered a fleet of merchant ships to be built. Then, for the first time, Israel became a sea-trading nation. Solomon's ships made his kingdom even richer than before. They traded in gold, silver, ivory, horses, apes, and monkeys.

Solomon was so rich that every day he ate out of golden bowls and plates, and drank out of golden cups. Even his clothes had golden threads sewn into the fabric.

Solomon's kingdom was very big. Israel and Judah stretched farther than at any other time. Former enemy tribes, such as the Philistines, brought gifts to Solomon. He was king over them, too. In order to make sure the land stayed protected, Solomon kept a strong army.

But above all, Solomon longed to judge the people with fairness. In one of his poems he wrote, "Teach the king to judge with righteousness. May he help the needy and crush people who take advantage of them.

Praise the Lord, who does wonderful things!" Solomon's heart's desire was to take good care of God's people. In this he was successful, as long as he followed God's laws.

The visit of the queen of Sheba

1 Kings 4.29–34; 10.1–13; 2 Chronicles 9.1–12

Word of Solomon's wealth and wisdom spread far and wide. He was wiser than all the wise men of the East and Egypt. People from all over the world came to hear the wisdom of Solomon. But one visitor was very special.

The queen of Sheba came from a distant land. This queen had heard of Solomon's greatness, but she didn't believe the stories. She journeyed a very long way to test him and see for herself if the stories were true.

The queen travelled with many camels, all carrying spices, gold, diamonds, and rubies. She came to Solomon and asked him every question she could think of.

Whether she asked about the habits of animals, plants, or the sea, or about the reasons for sorrow and joy, love and hatred, King Solomon knew the answers.

The wisdom which God gave Solomon had stretched his heart and mind. He could see a problem from all the different sides, and was then able to tell what was the right thing to do.

The queen said, "It was true what I heard in my own land about your words and your wisdom. In fact, they only told me half the truth — you are even wiser and richer than the stories I heard. I thank the Lord your God who made you king. He has given Israel a wonderful king!"

Then she gave Solomon many gifts of spices and precious stones. Never again would so many spices come into Israel at one time! She also gave Solomon a tremendous amount of gold. King Solomon gave the queen of Sheba many gifts as well.

Then the queen said farewell to King Solomon, and returned to her own land, far away. With her went even more tales of Solomon's wisdom. She had seen and heard it all with her own eyes and ears.

THE BIBLE'S LOVE SONG

A love song

Song of Solomon 1.1–8.14

There once were two people who were deeply in love. They thought of each other all the time, and wrote love poems for each other.

The man said, "How beautiful you are, my love; how your eyes shine with love."

"How handsome you are, my dearest," the woman replied. "How you delight me!"

The woman knew that her lover was strong, handsome, clever, and kind. The man loved the woman more than any other. He found her beautiful, and he cherished her.

It was spring-time, and the man said, "Come my love, my darling, come with me. The winter is over and the rains have stopped. In the countryside the flowers are in bloom. This is the time for singing, and the song of the doves is heard in the fields. Come, let me see your lovely face and hear your enchanting voice."

When they were apart they missed each other very much and longed for the time when they would be together again. They were sure of the love that they shared, and God had blessed them with eyes and hearts to see the best in each other. They promised themselves to each other, and nothing would destroy their true love.

What makes a good wife?

Proverbs 31.10–31

Part of being in love is seeing the good in the person you love. But no one is perfect, and when a man and woman fall in love they accept that each of them will have faults, yet they still love one another. They go on loving, even when times are hard. Here is some advice which was once given to a king by his mother.

"A good wife is hard to find. She is worth more than jewels. Her husband can trust her in everything because he knows she will always take care of him and their children. Her love for him will always make him happy.

"A good wife is always willing to work for her family. She can earn money and knows how to spend it wisely. She is not lazy but gets up early to take care of her children and her home. She is always ready for anything, in hard times or good, sunshine or snow.

"In all she says and does she is kind and wise. Her good heart is worth more than good looks and a made-up face. This woman's husband and children praise her and are proud of her. They appreciate all she does. "You are the best wife and mother in the world!" they tell her.

"But the most important thing is that this woman trusts the Lord, and lives as he wants her to. When a woman is like this, she deserves the respect of everyone."

LIFE CAN BE DIFFICULT

Solomon's mistake

1 Kings 11.1–13

As God had promised him, Solomon lived to become a very old man. But as he grew older he turned away from God. God no longer had the same place in his heart.

Solomon had hundreds of wives. Many of these wives were from tribes which used to be enemies of Israel. God had told his people not to marry people from other tribes because they worshipped different gods, and not the Lord. If God's people married these people then they might start worshipping their gods.

But Solomon married these women, and loved them. Through years of living with them and their worship, Solomon turned away from God, and worshipped foreign gods. He failed to love God with all his heart, as his father David had done. Instead he built altars and places of worship on high hills for other gods.

God had appeared to Solomon twice, and warned him not to worship any other gods. When Solomon did not listen, God was very angry.

The Lord said, "Because you have worshipped other gods and disobeyed my commands, I will take your kingdom away from you and give it to one of your officials." Because of God's promise to David that his family would always be kings, God said he would not do this in Solomon's lifetime, but in the lifetime of his son. He would also leave his son with one tribe, for the sake of David and Jerusalem. This was Solomon's punishment. Despite the wisdom, riches, and long life which God had given Solomon, he had chosen to do wrong, and needed to learn the importance of obeying God.

What is life all about?

Ecclesiastes 1.1–9.18

Sometimes life is good and enjoyable, as it was for Solomon while he obeyed God and had much wealth and much wisdom. At other times, however, it can be very difficult, as Solomon's son was going to discover.

In good times and bad times we find ourselves asking, "What is life all about? Why am I here, and what am I doing?"

These are the sorts of questions that the philosopher who wrote Ecclesiastes asked, too. A philosopher is someone who explores what life is about, and spends a lot of time thinking about it.

"It is useless," the philosopher said. "Everything is useless. The world goes on the same, day in and day out, and what does it all mean?" He thought that life was like chasing the wind – you could try your hardest, but you never got anywhere.

The philosopher set out to look for happiness. He looked for laughter, wisdom, possessions, and entertainment. He looked for greatness, and worked hard to make achievements. But still he couldn't find peace of mind.

He realized that all these things would be left behind when he died. What good would that do him? He had hoped that wisdom would bring happiness, but it didn't. The more he understood, the sadder it made him because it meant he had more to worry about.

The philosopher knew that God was in control of life, but he couldn't understand why there was so much suffering. He wondered why good people weren't always rewarded with happy lives, and why poor people were allowed to stay poor.

"What does it all mean?" he asked.

The meaning of life

Ecclesiastes 10.1—12.14

The philosopher noticed that often foolish people did well in the world, while wise people were ignored. "It doesn't make sense," he said.

Yet he saw that there were good things to enjoy in life — food, friends, and being young. "Enjoy being young," he said, "and remember that God wants you to love him and do what he wants. Don't let things worry you or make you upset. You aren't young for very long."

Because the philosopher was wise he kept on trying to understand what life was about. He continued to teach people what he knew. He was always honest as he tried to find answers, and never made up an answer just to be comforting.

"There is only one thing to say," the philosopher said. "Respect God and obey his commands, because that is what we are created for."

This would have been a good thing for King Solomon to remember as he sat thinking about what God had said to him. He hadn't obeyed God's commands, so most of his kingdom would go to another family.

A DIVIDED LAND

The punishment for Solomon's sins

1 Kings 11.14–43

As part of Solomon's punishment for
worshipping other gods, the Lord ended the
stability he had given to Solomon's kingdom.
He allowed the leaders of enemy tribes to
grow stronger.

One of these enemies was a man named Hadad. His tribe had almost been destroyed by Solomon's father, King David. But Hadad had escaped to Egypt and waited there until David died. Then he returned home and was made king of Edom. He was a very evil man, waiting for his chance to attack the Israelite kingdom.

Another enemy of Solomon was a leader of a gang of outlaws called Rezon. He had been made king of Syria, and hated Solomon and the Israelites.

Lastly, one of Solomon's own servants turned against him. His name was Jeroboam. He was visited by the prophet Ahijah. Ahijah wore a new cloak for the occasion. When he saw Jeroboam, he took off his cloak and tore it into twelve pieces. Then he gave ten of the pieces to Jeroboam.

"Here," Ahijah said, "the Lord says you will become ruler over ten of the twelve tribes of Israel, just as you hold these ten pieces of my cloak in your hand."

As God had warned Solomon, his kingdom would be taken from the hands of his son, and given to one of his officials. But Solomon's son was not to lose all the kingdom. Because of God's promises to David, Judah would remain in the hands of Solomon's son, and continue to be ruled by the family of David.

The prophet said, "This is because God has chosen Jerusalem, the capital of Judah, as his city." Jerusalem was where the temple of the Lord stood.

When King Solomon heard about this he tried to kill Jeroboam, so Jeroboam ran away to Egypt where he stayed until Solomon died.

It was while his enemies were becoming stronger that the great King Solomon died. He had ruled over Israel for forty years and God kept all his promises to him, having given him deep wisdom, riches, and a long life. But by the time Solomon died, his kingdom was beginning to show signs of weakness because he had chosen not to follow God alone.

The new king makes the wrong choice

1 Kings 12.1–18; 2 Chronicles 10.1–19

After Solomon's death his son Rehoboam became king. When Jeroboam heard this he returned to Israel, and he and the people who lived in the northern part of Israel went to their new king to ask a very important question.

They said, "Your father King Solomon always made us work too hard on all his building projects. Please, as you are the new king, will you lighten the burden he placed on our shoulders, so we won't have to work so hard?"

While Solomon was king he had many palaces and forts built, and while his slaves did most of the work, much was also done by his own people.

Rehoboam told them he would think about it for three days, then give them his answer. So Rehoboam asked the wise advisers of his father what he should do. "Go ahead," they said. "Lighten their loads and then they will serve you all their lives."

But then Rehoboam asked his young friends who had grown up with him and who were his new advisers. They said, "Make the people work even harder. Make them wish they worked for Solomon again."

Rehoboam chose to listen to his friends. When the three days were over he told the people, "No! You can't work less hard. In fact, you will have to work harder for me than you ever did for my father."

All the people booed and hissed at King Rehoboam. "Down with David's family!" they shouted. "We want nothing to do with you!"

King Rehoboam called his man who was in charge of forcing the people to work. "Make them obey me!" he said. But when this man went into the crowd, they went mad with anger and killed him. Then the king saw what a big mistake he had made. He mounted his

chariot and rode as fast as he could, all the way back to Jerusalem.

The land is split

1 Kings 12.19–33; 2 Chronicles 11.1–17
When the tribes of Israel who lived in the northern part of the land saw this, they called Jeroboam and asked him to be their king.

"We want Jeroboam!" they said. "Make Jeroboam king!" Only Judah in the south remained loyal to Solomon's son Rehoboam, just as the prophet had said. Everyone else wanted Jeroboam.

When Rehoboam heard this, he called all his soldiers together to make war against the tribes of Israel. But a man of God came to him and said, "The Lord says you are not to go into battle against your relatives, members of the same nation. Tell all your men to go home."

Rehoboam remembered how his father King Solomon had taught him to listen to the Lord, so he obeyed. For several years afterwards he followed the Lord's teachings and encouraged his people to do the same. All the people who believed in God and followed his ways moved to Jerusalem so they could worship the Lord there, under the protection of King Rehoboam.

They did this because the other king, Jeroboam, had done a very evil thing. He would not let the priests worship the Lord, but appointed priests of his own to worship pagan gods. He tried to push the people away from God and towards worshipping these false gods. The Lord's priests did not obey Jeroboam. Instead they all moved to Jerusalem to worship the one, true God.

But the damage was done. Because Solomon had done wrong, and because God's people began to worship other gods, the nation split into the northern tribes of Israel and the southern tribe of Judah. Already many had forgotten how important it was to love and obey God, and live as God wanted them to. Yet God had remembered his promise to King David, and his family was still on the throne of Judah in Jerusalem, worshipping the Lord.

Adventure Story Bible   Old Testament

New Testament